# The Hack-Proof Password System

Protect Yourself Online

With a Memory Expert's

In-Depth Guide to Remembering

Passwords

Brad Zupp

Simply Sensible Entertainment, Inc.
**The Hack-Proof Password System**
Protect Yourself Online With a Memory Expert's
In-Depth Guide to Remembering Passwords

Published in the United States of America by Simply
Sensible Entertainment, Inc.
ISBN 978-0-9899547-3-0

# Table of Contents

Brad Zupp is a motivational speaker, memory improvement expert, and author. Since 2009, he has been dedicated to testing the limits of his own memory while helping tens of thousands of people learn the benefits that come from memory improvement and exercising the mind. Brad shows people how to supercharge their memories to improve cyber security, sales, relationships, productivity, and peace of mind.

He is also a frequent memory sports competitor, and has won two bronze and one silver medal at memory competitions. He has twice set an American record at world memory championships.

Brad hasn't always had a world-class memory. When he turned 40, he noticed a sharp decline in his memory abilities. Determined to not live with a "natural" memory decline as he aged, he threw himself into memory improvement and discovered the "secret" that he now shares with audiences worldwide: memory improvement is possible. It can be easy, and even fun.

At age 48, Brad's memory is sharper than ever. He's living proof that we don't have to struggle to remember secure passwords, feel the embarrassed that comes when we forget the names of people we meet, miss appointments, rely on notes for speeches, or forget what our families, friends, and coworkers tell us.

Brad accomplishments include:
- Memorized the names of 117 people in 15 minutes
- Set the American record — twice — for memorizing digits spoken at one number per second, never read or reviewed
- Memorized 10.5 decks of shuffled playing cards perfectly in one hour
- Memorized one deck of shuffled playing cards in 58 seconds
- Memorized 1,250 binary digits (100110101101...) in 30 minutes

He has been featured on *The Today Show*, *Fox News New York*, *The Dr. Steve Show*, *The Dr. Joy Show*, and in *USA Today*, *The LA Times*, and newspapers worldwide.

For more information about Brad's keynote speeches, seminars, coaching, or memory improvement tips, visit www.BradZupp.com or email: Brad@BradZupp.com. He can also be found on Twitter: @BradZupp and Facebook: www.facebook.com/FeatsOfMemory. You may also be interested in Brad's other book: *Unlock Your Amazing Memory*.

# Part 1: The Tools

# 1
# *Why Create Secure Passwords?*

**Memorable Versus Strong**

How secure are your passwords? How well do you remember them? The problem is that our ability to remember passwords is in direct opposition to how strong they should be. When we make strong passwords, we have a hard time remembering them. We tend to write them down or store them somewhere, making them weaker than they should be. On the other hand, we purposefully use weak passwords because they are easy to recall.

**Startling Statistics**

Weak passwords account for approximately 76% of attacks on corporate networks.

51% of adults in the United States suffered a security incident in 2015.

Facebook has 600,000+ accounts compromised per day.

40% of IT departments store passwords — including admin passwords — in a document or spreadsheet on a company computer.

## How vulnerable are you to hacking?

Test yourself:

1. Do you use completely unique passwords for *every* website?
2. Are all of your passwords *at least* 12 characters long?
3. Do your passwords avoid the format of word(s) plus two digits?
4. Do you avoid using the name of your pet or partner plus a number for a password?
5. Have you used any password longer than 24 months?
6. Have you changed your password on Yahoo, LinkedIn, Dropbox, Twitter, Weebly, Target, Home Depot, Tumblr, Myspace, and others after they have been hit by data breaches?

7. Do you login to your bank or investment accounts online?
8. Do you shop online?
9. Does any website have your credit card information saved?
10. Would you be embarrassed if either a stranger or someone you knew read one of your private emails?
11. Have you ever shared an opinion about someone else via email that would upset them to read it?
12. Would your job be in jeopardy if your work email or business login were compromised?
13. Would it be time-consuming, difficult, costly, frustrating, or annoying to recover a hacked social media or email account?

If you answered no to any of the questions from 1-6, or yes to any of the questions from 7-13, you're vulnerable. You need to learn how to protect yourself immediately. This book is the answer. With some basic knowledge plus a bit of imagination, you will make yourself and your personal data safer on the internet by knowing how to create and remember more secure passwords.

Don't be oblivious to the dangers. According to a report in *Business Insider*, 90% of all passwords are vulnerable to hacking because users can't remember them.

We use passwords that could easily be guessed by anyone who knows us well, like the name of our pet with a number after it. We think we're clever when we replace "S" with "$" or "L" with a "1," but we're shocked — *shocked!* — when someone gets into our online backup, email, or bank account. We use easy-to-remember passwords that are so common it would be funny, if it wasn't so sad, like actual passwords from a list compiled from files containing millions of stolen passwords posted online:

    12345678
    abc123
    qwerty
    admin
    ncc1701
    password1
    trustno1

What happens when a hacker steals all the passwords and user names for a company's website, as has happened often in the last few years? The hackers take the information and program their computers to hit millions of other computers, using the username and password combination to see who uses the same for multiple websites. Presto — they're now in your other accounts, merely because you struggle to remember passwords.

**Why don't we try to remember?**

**"My browser does it for me."** This is helpful, except when you lose your computer or it gets stolen, or merely left unattended. What about when your browser cache gets cleared and you lose all the stored information? What happens when you have to login from a different computer?

**"I have password software that does it for me."** In July 2015, a popular password software company's computer system was attacked, with hackers making off with users' email addresses, the reminders used to retrieve passwords, and data about people's master passwords. The company reported that the master passwords appeared to be encrypted, not in plain text, hopefully limiting the exposure. Also, what happens if you forget your long, ultra-secure main password? Did you memorize it, or is it written down, stuck to your computer monitor?

**"I just write them down on a piece of paper Who's going to try to break in, or try to hack me?"** Identity theft by people known to the victim is common. Whether it's an untrustworthy spouse, coworker, visitor, or acquaintance, that sticky note with your passwords sitting by your computer, in your desk drawer, or — I've seen it with my own eyes — taped to the underside of the laptop, is like waving a red cape at an angry bull.

**"I just use the same password everywhere. It'll all work out, I'm not worried."** Sure, the bank or online shop may catch unusual activity on your account, but how quickly? How much time will it cost you to fix it?

**"I have a horrible memory."** Now we're getting somewhere! This is the real issue, the one that is at the root of all the other excuses. If remembering secure, hard-to-hack passwords was easy, would we need any of the excuses above? No. But remembering the passwords would have to be easy and foolproof. Is that possible? Yes. Read on.

**Why bother to remember passwords?**

1. It's more secure. No one can hack your mind.
2. Exercising your memory keeps your mind sharp and makes it easier to remember other essentials, like what a loved one says, what your client or manager tells you, where you put your keys, or the name of a person you met.
3. Remembering passwords can be easy and even fun, if you do it right.

Let's get to the root of the problem. Many of us struggle to remember ordinary things like the names of people we meet or where we parked our car. It's especially difficult to recall random words and numbers strung together. Passwords might as well be words in a foreign language that we don't speak or understand.

Computer security experts insist we need a different, unique password for every single website. At my last count, I have approximately 80 website passwords, which isn't unusual. We're frequently asked to create a password for yet another login, and also to change the old ones because they've 'expired.' How can we possibly manage so many passwords, keeping them all straight, while still making them difficult to hack?

**The good and bad news: no one has ever shown us how to create and remember secure passwords.**

This is an area where my unique skills come in handy. I'm a memory improvement expert. I have one of the best memories in the world, but it wasn't always like that. When I was younger I couldn't remember numbers at all. Do you remember calling 411 ("Information") to get a phone number? I could never recall a phone number long enough to hang up and call it. And that was back when phone numbers were only seven digits!

When I turned 40, I realized my already poor memory was getting worse. I wondered if an ordinary guy could improve his memory with effort. I threw myself into memory improvement, learning all I could, training my memory, testing myself, developing my own tricks and techniques. My memory improved.

My memory got so much better that I set a USA record two years in a row at the world championships of memory. At — get this — the Spoken Numbers event. A computerized voice recites a series of numbers, one digit per second. They can't be seen or written down. I memorized 112 in a row perfectly one year, then broke my own record the next year with 150 digits with no mistakes. Imagine listening to the operator reading out 15 ten-digit phone numbers, one after another, and memorizing all of them after hearing them only once. That's what I did.

To say that my memory improved is a huge understatement. However, despite developing my memory abilities to a world-class level, I still struggled with remembering passwords. What was wrong? For years this was my dark secret.

Eventually, enough was enough. After one too many times of clicking the "Forgot Password?" button, I decided to take what I knew about memory improvement and develop a password system for myself. I looked at all the reasons I was forgetting passwords, where I was going wrong, and how I could fix it. Finally, after a lot of trial and error, I had a system which worked. It used more characters — enough to make the passwords secure. It avoided all the common password formats. It even worked for randomly assigned passwords like "6jKY4PxdHM$LNrcf".

Best of all, it made passwords easy to remember. It worked in the real world. I went from using passwords that were too short and easily hacked — but easy to remember — to using strong passwords, that were also easy to remember.

If I can do it, you can too. You can improve your memory and use this system to create and recall more secure passwords. All you need is some pointers, which you'll learn in this book. Don't worry, you won't have to do anything like my feats of memory to easily memorize passwords.

No matter your age or background, by working through this book you will:
1. Understand how we remember passwords, and why we forget them.
2. Learn "The Steps of Memory."
3. Discover "The Three Keys to Remembering Anything."
4. Develop your own, custom system for imagining passwords.
5. Learn three distinct methods for creating passwords.
6. Strengthen your creativity.
7. Finally be able to remember passwords.

**The Learning Curve**

There is a learning curve to being able to memorize more secure passwords, the same as there is for doing many worthwhile things in life. First we learn to crawl, then walk, then ride a bicycle, then drive a car. Why? We want to be able to reach our destinations more easily and quickly. If you grow up in a big city, where there are plenty of mass transit options available, perhaps you decide learning to drive isn't necessary: it's costly and time consuming to learn, and there are easier options available.

The same is true for passwords. Is it worth the effort? Only you can decide, but here are several arguments for taking the time:

1. We use passwords all the time, so the small amount of effort to learn a system is worth the time investment.
2. Learning how to memorize passwords will improve your creativity, focus, and memory for other areas of your life.
3. Having  more secure passwords could save you money, headache, and time. Instead of getting hacked, you stay secure.
4. Believe it or not, memorizing passwords can be fun!
5. Exercising your mind by learning these techniques may keep your mind sharper and healthier as you age.

# 2
## *The Steps of Memory*

## The Steps of Memory

Before we jump into creating and memorizing passwords, we have to figure out where we're having the most trouble by looking at "The Steps of Memory." Remembering has three distinct steps. We have to get up all three steps to get the prize: the memory. Knowing which area we need to work on will make the process of memory improvement easier.

We may get tripped up on different steps in different areas of our lives.

At work we may be very focused and have no trouble getting the information. We pay attention to what our clients or managers tell us, we listen attentively on conference calls, we read emails carefully. Nothing goes 'in one ear and out the other.'

When we do this, the information **gets** into our minds, our natural memory abilities take over, and we remember. We automatically **save** the information... unless we're overwhelmed.

With so much data coming at us, so many tasks and things to keep track of, we often lose the information we are so careful to get. We later can't recall something important because too much flooded in at once. This is the result of not having a system of organizing the information efficiently in our minds.

There are other times when we're put on the spot and suddenly have a 'senior moment' or 'brain freeze.' We know the information but can't access it. "It's on the tip of my tongue," we say. After a few moments, the memory may pop into our mind, but unfortunately, it's often too late. We're embarrassed and wonder what our problem is. That's tripping on the last step: **recall**.

At home, it may be another story. Our children, friends, family, and our partners tell us many things. We've worked hard all day and our brains just need a break. We often find ourselves tuning out, not putting in the effort to focus and **get** the information.

Later, we don't remember what we were told, or we realize that we forgot someone's birthday or our anniversary, or we forget to pick up something from the store on the way home or that our mother-in-law was stopping by.

We didn't "forget" — *we never got the information in the first place.*

Often when it's time to create and remember a new password, we have a lot going on. We attempt to log into a new website and we are told we have to register and create a password. In the middle of our busy day (whether at work or home), we need to:

- Stop
- Create a unique password that we'll remember
- Check our email for a confirmation link
- Realize it's not there
- Wait, looking at other websites in the meantime
- Check our email again
- Check the spam folder
- Wonder why we haven't gotten the confirmation link
- Realize that we have just received it
- Click on the link
- Re-enter our username and password (assuming we still remember both) and then
- Go on our way to accomplish what we wanted to do when confronted with the registration process.

There is plenty of room for tripping over the steps in this process.

1. GET: We're distracted by the sign-up process, in a hurry, or focused on accomplishing what we're on the website for. We're not focused on memorizing a password.
2. SAVE: We don't organize the password in our minds to make it simple to recover later.
3. RECALL: Days, weeks, or months from the time we sign up, we're back on the website and need to login again, only to blank out.

Did we pay enough attention to encode it from the start ("Get")? Have we forgotten because it's not organized well in our mind (the "Save" step)? Will we remember later, when there's no pressure ("Recall")? But by then we've already changed the password to something else!

Some would say it doesn't matter what step we tripped on. We can't remember it, so the end result is the same. I think it's essential to identify the problem so we can fix the issue. We also need to ensure that all areas are working well, because it just takes one missed step to make us forget.

## The Solution

From now on, every time you create a new password, you will follow a plan to:
1. Focus and **get** the password.
2. **Save** it by organizing it in your mind in a way that will make it easy to eventually recall it next time you need it.
3. Practice **recall** to cement the memory in your mind.

Can you do it? Yes, you've got this. It's much easier than you think. You already have an amazing memory. Think of all the things you know and remember. It's absolutely astounding. You only need some strategies, a system, and a little practice so passwords become one of the many things that easily stick in your mind. This process will help accomplish that.

# 3
## *The Three Keys to Remembering Anything*

**How to Remember**

Many of us were told in school that the way to remember something difficult was to "read it again." It didn't matter that we read and re-read the material until we were bored and discouraged. Brute force repetition was the key. "Try harder," we heard.

The good and bad news is that brute force repetition — repeating something over and over — will make it stick in your mind. But at what cost? It's frustrating, boring, and the memories created tend to fade quickly. There's nothing to hold them in our minds for the long term.

Passwords are no different than our boring schoolwork was. We try to force the information to stick in our minds by brute force, which is boring but works... for a while. If we have to enter a password repeatedly every day — to unlock the desktop screen, for example — we can learn it quickly and retain it well. If we let our browser remember a password for us from the start, it will probably be gone by the next time we need it.

What we weren't taught in school is a simple, fun technique to memorizing. One that uses the natural way our minds prefer to remember. We tap into our creativity and work with our minds to make password memorization easier and — dare I say it — fun.

## The Memory Detective

We each have a "memory detective" in our minds. Our memory detective wants to "solve the case" by recalling the details we need to make us look good. Our job is to give the detective a few clues. The rest is up to them.

Some clues are better than others, just like on those melodramatic television shows. A photo or video of what happened makes the case easier to solve than a smudged boot print or spec of dirt. To our memory detective, a picture or video is the same as it is to the television detective, because our minds love pictures. Scientists have done studies that show our minds remember pictures very well.

## The Three Keys to Remembering Anything

We'll use what scientists have discovered to work *with* our minds, not against them. I created these Three Keys to Remembering Anything.

This is the process that makes memorizing easy. With a small amount of practice, it will become second nature.

Key #1: Picture

Translate whatever you need to remember into a picture. Your memory detective will love it and remember it more easily than simply reading the material over and over.

Key #2: Connect

Connect two or more pictures together, like linked paper clips, or a paper clip holding pieces of paper together.

Key #3: Review

Add detail as you review the image or movie you created.

Let's try a simple example before we apply this technique to memorizing passwords.

## Spelling

When we have trouble spelling, we usually know almost the whole word, but have trouble with just a certain part. For example, that yummy green vegetable we should eat more of:

Brocolli
Broccolli
Brocholi
Broccoli
Bracholi
Bracholli

One of those is spelled correctly. Do you know which one? It's "Broccoli." For years I spelled this incorrectly, always having trouble with the middle part. "Is it one 'C' or two?" I'd invariable ask myself. "Wait, maybe it's 'ch'?"

Let's use the Keys.

### Picture

We need to picture broccoli. That's easy. Imagine a big, yummy bunch of broccoli, all green and fresh. If you hate the taste, it may be even easier to picture. Think of a lot of broccoli that you have to eat.

Next, we need to picture "C" — but not the letter. We need to translate "C" into something that we can easily see in our minds. What does "C" remind you of? Cowboys? Clowns? Cake? Cookies? Whatever it is, picture two of them, representing the two "C"s in broccoli.

### Connect

Create a story that ties everything together. Here are a few ideas:

- Two cowboys are roasting broccoli over their camp fire out on the range.
- Two clowns are fighting over which one gets to eat the broccoli.

- Your best friend made you not one, but *two*, broccoli cakes for your birthday.
- You make your grandkid two broccoli cookies as a treat.

Next, take two seconds to close your eyes and create this scene in your mind. Don't just read this and think, "Interesting, I can see how that works." **Do the exercise!**

### Review
Take a few extra seconds to add details and review your image or movie. What color are the cowboys' hats? Are the clowns friendly or scary? Are the cakes or cookies green, or tan with green broccoli chunks? How do they taste?

That's the middle of the word. If you also have trouble spelling the end, you could picture one of the clowns or cowboys 'l'eaving with the broccoli while the other stays, disappointed and hungry. Your grandchild 'l'aughs at you and refuses the cookies. The broccoli cakes have 'l'ime slices on top as decoration. Turn "L" into a picture and add it to the story.

I bet I know what you're thinking. Either that this is too easy and won't work, too difficult for you to use, or just too strange. Hang in there. Your memory detective loves this and you'll be remembering the strongest passwords in no time if you give this a chance.

## Make It Memorable

The Three Keys to Remembering Anything work better if we can tap into our creative side. As we get older, we often lose our creative side. It's like our 'funny bone' is broken. We need to fix that broken funny bone by putting a CAST on it.

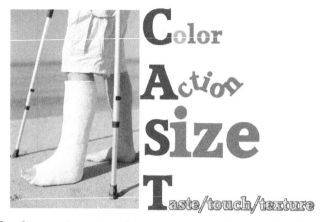

**C**olor
**A**ction
**S**ize
**T**aste/touch/texture

Add color, action, size (bigger, not smaller), and either taste, touch, or texture to your images as you create and review them. For me, one is enough, but if something isn't sticking in your mind, add as many as needed. Making your images, stories or movies more creative like this will make them even easier to remember. (Yes, your broken funny bone isn't in your leg, but a picture that is incorrect can be easier to remember than one that makes sense.)

Now that you understand the fundamentals, it's time to practice all the memory techniques before we move on to creating and memorizing passwords.

# 4
## *Memory Practice*
## *Part 1*

**Practice**

As with any new skill, practice is essential.

To practice your creativity and Picture, Connect, Review, we'll use a simple memory exercise that will prove very hand in the next section.

**Exercise #1: Creativity**

For this practice, it's great if you have a timer on a watch or phone. Set if for five minutes. If you don't have one, however, estimate five minutes.

Look at the list of words below. Use the Picture, Connect, and Review keys with each pair.

Picture one word, then picture the other. Connect the two in a creative story using color, action, size, and taste, touch, or texture. Make your connections creative and fun.

Get through as many as you can in the five-minute time limit.

Computer / Saw

Flag / Tree

Tennis ball / Coffee cup

Television / Fly

Boat / Windmill

Bird / Straw

Snow / Skateboard

King / Cave

Swim / Car

Trip / Slow

Cloud / Late

Annoying / Lucky

Seeds / Cavity

Staircase / Heavy

Host / Muffin

Moon / Happiness

Pilot / Photograph

Camel / Frame

Rent / Decade

Dove / Bench

Sandwich / Child

Garbage / Canoe

Did you find some easier than others to picture? Generally, it's easier to mentally picture an object than an idea. For "Rent," you may have pictured an apartment. For "Happiness," you may have thought of someone you know who is happy, or a smiling face. No matter what word or idea, you can picture it if you take a second and use your imagination.

Next, were you careful to add detail? If we're just reading, the images pop into our minds and we move on. For remembering later, it's important to take the extra half second to think, "What color do I want my camel to be? How about green? No... pink. Even better: pink and green!" It's not only okay to be silly, it's encouraged.

The skill of first creating a mental image, creating another image, then connecting them together, is a worthy one to develop. The more you practice, the easier it gets. Next, we'll learn the technique behind creating and memorizing secure passwords and use this skill to make them easy to remember.

# 5
## *Memory Practice*
## *Part 2*

**Quiz**

Before we continue, it's time for a quiz. Part of recall is testing ourselves. As we get used to accessing information in our minds more than before, we train our minds to pay better attention.

Without referring to the past section, recall as many word pairs as possible. Take as long as you need.

Computer   _____

Flag   _____

Tennis ball   _____

Television   _____

Boat   _____

Bird   _____

Snow   _____

King   _____

Swim   _____

Trip   _____

Cloud   _____

Annoying   _____

Seeds   _____

Staircase   _____

Host   _____

Moon   _____

Pilot   _____

Camel   _____

Rent   _____

Dove   _____

Sandwich   _____

Garbage   _____

How many did you remember easily? How many took

some effort?

If you missed any, consider *why* you forgot them. Was it difficult to picture one of the words in the pair, or both? Did the connection not come together easily? Did you skip the Review step? Did you not bother to use CAST?

Analyze where you struggled so when you're sitting in front of your computer, trying to memorize a password for a new site, you make sure you do what is needed to make the images stick.

# Part 2:

# Remembering Passwords

# 6

# *About Passwords*

## Common Scenarios

There are several ways passwords are stolen or hacked. Some we can avoid by having more secure passwords, but some we can't.

**Phishing** is a general attack on a large group of people. We receive an email, phone call, or text message that seems legitimate, but is actually from hackers. We are instructed to provide or reset our password or to provide other information like a credit card number. Having a secure password doesn't do any good if we provide it upon request, or login with our old password and create a new one on the fake website, thereby giving hackers our old password to use on the actual site. The best method for avoiding this is to never provide a password unless you type in the address to your website directly, instead of following a link, and to be suspicious of people who request personal information no matter how reputable they or the email seems.

**Spear Phishing** is a more specific attack on you. First, hackers research details about your life: your friends, hobbies, employer, where you're from, and the places you go. Then they disguise themselves as a friend or trusted person or company in an attempt to get your password, credit card number, or other important information. This is generally done through instant messages or email. The contact seems more personal and there is a level of knowledge about you that makes it seem more legitimate.

Having secure passwords does little to help in these situations, except for one huge factor. If you use unique passwords for every single login, you're much safer. If you're tricked by a phishing or spear phishing attack, your password is compromised only for that particular website. All of your other sites are safe. No one can use the hacked password, or try to figure out slight variations, on other websites.

### Website Hack

Another common scenario is that a website you use is hacked and the user information is stolen. If the website has even the most basic internal security, your username and password are stored in an encrypted format (though this isn't always the case.) Some websites use weaker encryption than others, allowing hackers to use sophisticated software, plus dictionaries and databases of common passwords and password formats to decrypt your password, along with all the others in the batch (often tens of thousands). Then the hackers have your username and password, allowing them to attempt to use that combination on other sites. Once again, having a unique password for each website is essential. Having a password of sufficient length, with an uncommon format, also makes your password harder to figure out than the other thousands the hackers' computers are decrypting.

### Untrustworthy People

An all-too-common problem is an untrustworthy person hacking or figuring out our password and using it to embarrass, steal from us, or wreak havoc in our lives. Having secure passwords helps tremendously here. If an ex-partner or former friend knows how much you love your pet and that you use some variation of its name for all your passwords, you are vulnerable to their unscrupulous behavior. (Using a pet name or other easily-guessed word or phrase also makes simpler for a stranger to employ a spear phishing attack.) Unique passwords help tremendously in this scenario.

### Malicious Software

Some software or online apps can hijack social media accounts or corrupt your computer. Be wary of clicking on links to new apps or software without vetting it first. Don't rely on your friends on social media: it's too easy for one friend or family member to do something wrong, then follow in their footsteps because they must know best, when they don't. Check it yourself to make sure your accounts or system doesn't get hijacked.

### Best Practices

First we'll learn what we need to do to create secure passwords, then we'll learn how to remember them. Here are the essential rules for passwords.

1. Never use the same password for more than one site. **Ever**.
2. Don't use slight variations of the same password on more than one site.
3. Use a **minimum** of 12 characters.
4. Use upper- and lowercase letters.
5. A longer password — even without upper- and lowercase letters, numbers, or special characters — tends to be more secure than a shorter, complex password.
6. Avoid any word that is easily related to you: the name of a pet, child, family member, or close friend; or phrases like

'gonefishing' and "TGIF."

7. Avoid common words for passwords, like the names of sports teams or famous players.

8. Avoid common formats, like a word or name followed by a two digit number.

9. Never save a password to your computer in a text file, even in a hidden or disguised way.

How do your current passwords compare to these recommendations? If following these rules seems daunting, relax. We've got this covered.

# 7
## *Password Creation Methods*

There are two methods for creating secure yet memorable passwords. (There is a separate method for remembering passwords that are assigned to you, which we'll cover after this section.)

Both involve using our imaginations to connect thoughts to other thoughts. This is working with our minds. We'll use The Three Keys to Remembering Anything extensively, so if you don't recall what they are, review that section. Make sure you've done the word pairing exercises (and test) before proceeding.

The Three Keys to Remembering Anything work because our mind remembers pictures well. Also, from the time we're babies, we hear and love stories. When we're young, we hear stories about our family histories. We tell our family what we did that day and the story of our exciting adventures. Later in life, we tell the story of how we met our partner, what happened on vacation, or how our day went. We already know how to picture ideas, remember them, and tell stories, so we'll use the same techniques to create and remember passwords.

Passwords are everywhere. We have to create and memorize them whether we want to or not. Since we have to remember so many of them so often, we might as well take the time to do it easily and well.

Both password creation methods use words that are easily translated into pictures and linked together into an image or mental movie. Since you're creating the password, you get to pick the images and make them as interesting (and memorable) as you want.

The first method uses words alone and is called the Word Chain Method. The second method uses words that are combined into a phrase, then reduced down to an easy-to-remember but obscure looking password. It's called the Phrase Chain Method. My recommendation is the Word Chain Method, but some people naturally prefer the Phrase Chain Method. You will learn both, then decide for yourself which seems more suitable for you.

# 8

# *The Word Chain Method*

**Example: The Word Chain Method In Action**

A few years ago, we bought new carpet for our home. To track of the status of the order, we had to create an account on the website of the carpet vendor, which was a big-box home improvement store.

"Great," I thought, rolling my eyes as I sat at my computer. "Another password to remember. When am I ever going to login to this site after our carpet purchase is complete?" Even though our credit card information wasn't on file, I still wanted the password to be difficult to hack, easy to remember, and different from any other passwords I had.

My method? I used the Three Keys to Remembering Anything. Picture. Connect. Review.

First, I pictured the store. I would be on their website the next time I needed to recall the password, and I'd naturally think of the company and store. That would be my anchor.

Next, when I thought about the store, what came to mind? I thought about the lumber they sell and the color of the store's logo, but since the carpet was such a big purchase, I decided to use the idea of the carpet as the first link in the password story chain. Whenever I went back to the site in the future, I figured the expensive carpet purchase would pop into my head, so "carpet" would be the first word.

Now I had a new starting point. Instead of the hardware store, I had carpet. What could I picture that would easily come to mind when I thought of it? We picked that particular carpet because it was noticeably softer than the other choices. "Soft" would be my next link in the chain.

Besides soft, it was beige, which went with everything in the house. It also had little flecks of color in it to hide dirt in between times we vacuumed.

My final password was "CarpetSoftBeigeFlecks". I decided to capitalize the first letter of each word, which isn't very original, but it makes sense to me. (We'll discuss your personal system for capitalization and where to add numbers in another chapter.)

How strong is this password, according to an online password checker? Excellent. 100% strength, plenty of characters, uppercase and lowercase letters. However, no numbers and no symbols. Is it good enough? Yes. It would take a "botnet" — a huge group of computers working together — about 4 quadrillion years to hack it. Is it the strongest password I could create? Not at all. Adding numbers and symbols would help. Still, for a site that doesn't have my account information, it's great.

## Method #1: The Word Chain Method

The above example gives you an idea of how we're going to create better passwords that are easy to remember. Let's go through the steps one by one, examine a few examples, then practice some of your own.

We create a series of pictures and link them together, like links in a chain, or scenes from a movie. Remember the process of The Three Keys to Remembering Anything?

### Picture

1. Select your anchor.

Your anchor is the first clue for your memory detective. Normally this is the website or company you are creating the password for. It could be your school, your email account, shopping site, or even your computer itself. Whatever comes to mind when you think of the website, you convert into a picture.

### Connect

2. Create the first link.

What does the anchor remind you of? Picture that. This is link one in your chain or the first scene of your movie. Combine the image of the anchor with the image of link one using at least one portion of CAST to make it more memorable.

3. Create the second link.

What does link one remind you of? Picture that, and add it to the picture, story, or movie created by combining the anchor and link one.

4. Create the third link.

Repeat as needed until you have at least 12 characters. My recommendation is at least 20 characters, as long as that many is allowed by the website. Adding a few extra links won't make the process more difficult.

### Review

5. Review the story you've created. Add color, action, size, and taste, texture, or touch to links of the chain to solidify the memory.

## Remember the Process

It may seem slower at first, but this is actually "AFSTR" ("a faster") way to memorize passwords. Use the AFSTR acronym to help remember the process:

**A**(nchor)
**F**(irst) link
**S**(econd) link
**T**(hird) link
**R**(epeat) and/or **R**(eview)

## Exercise #2: Statue of Liberty Website

Let's try one that's fun, using something we can all relate to.

For some reason, we have to create a password to login to the Statue of Liberty website.

1. Select the **a**nchor. Let's use the image of Lady Liberty herself. When we go to the website and have to enter our password, that's the obvious thing we'll think of. Picture the anchor. Luckily, it's easy to picture the Statue of Liberty.

2. Create the **f**irst link. What comes to mind when you think of the Statue of Liberty? This is where discernment comes

in. We don't want to use this technique to make it easy for hackers, so we have to pick something obvious to us but not obvious to others.

Obvious: green, torch, France, New York. All of these are generic to some degree and are okay to use if you must.

Less obvious: break down the words or ideas. When you think of "liberty," what do you think of? A favorite president? A date in history? When you think of "statue," what comes to mind? Bronze? Michaelangelo's *David*? Instead of thinking about the Statue of Liberty in New York City, did you think of the smaller recreation in Las Vegas? Any of these are excellent to use.

Unique to me: 1985, my friend Steve, claustrophobia, long line, messenger. All of these came to mind immediately when I thought of the Statue of Liberty, for reasons that are personal to me. (Though anyone who has taken the boat trip to the island has waited in a long line, or if you've walked up the stairs inside the statue you might have experienced claustrophobia.)

Find a balance between obvious and obscure. Anything unique to you is better because it's not only harder for someone else to guess, but also is easier for you to recall.

For this example, use New York. Picture an apple (New York is known as "The Big Apple"). Connect the anchor with the first link. Combine an apple with the statue in a fun, silly way, using color, action, size, and touch, taste, or texture. Instead of holding up a torch, I see Lady Liberty holding up a huge, red, shiny apple.

3. Create the **s**econd link using the previous link as a starting point. Thinking of the apple, what does it remind you of?

What about a worm? Picture it and add it to the image. The worm wiggles out of the apple and scares everyone touring the island.

So far, we have for the Statue of Liberty website: appleworm. This is only nine characters and is too weak. Adding two capital letters helps: AppleWorm, but it's still too simple.

4.  Create the **t**hird link. What does "worm" remind you of? Fishing? Picture it: the worm wiggles away on the island, where a fisherman grabs it and attaches it to a giant fish hook. AppleWormFishing

The online password evaluation of "AppleWormFishing" is rated "Excellent," though it may still be too simple.

5. Now you can **r**epeat or **r**eview. If you add one more link, think of the size or type of fish that gets caught, or maybe have the fisherman reel in a tire instead. "AppleWormFishingThisBig!" or "AppleWormFishingTire!" would be great.

## Unique and Individual

It's harder for hackers to guess a password, and easier for us to remember it, when we use our personal experiences to create it. In our above Statue of Liberty example, I would have pictured Lady Liberty as the anchor, and my friend Steve as my first link. Steve and I worked together one day near the statue. I'd picture him looking across the water at the statue as the combination of the anchor and the first link.

Then, since he's a successful professional magician, I'd picture him throwing playing cards at the statue, with one of them chopping off the torch on the statue. That would get him arrested, and I'd go bail him out.

Statue of Liberty website: Stevecardstorchdarkbail. To make it better, I'd add the year we visited the park, plus capitalize some letters, making it "steve1986cardstorchdarkBAIL."

This is probably excessive for a website where no personal information is stored, but you get the idea of what can be done.

At first, this may seem difficult, especially if you're not used to being creative. It also takes an extra few seconds. But every time you use this technique, it will feel easier.

## Exercise #3: Television Password

Practice another one. Imagine that you have to enter a password to watch television. Create your password, using AFSTR method.

**A**nchor: The television.
**F**irst: When you think of television, what comes to mind? A favorite show or actor? Electricity? Family time? Select the most obvious one, knowing that you'll probably remember that next time as well. Connect it to the television by picturing watching that show or actor, etc.
**S**econd: What does the first link remind you of? Picture it and add it to the story. Make sure it's memorable by using CAST.
**T**hird: What does the second link remind you of? Picture that and add it to the story.
**R**eview by adding details, especially size and action, which are the two that work best for most people.

Here's what I thought of: WaltJessieEmpireDead. (I've

been watching *Breaking Bad* reruns.)

> Strength: 100%
> Evaluation: Excellent
> Length: 20 characters
> Good: Upper- and lowercase letters used.
> Bad: No numbers or symbols.
> Estimated time to hack: 81 trillion years.

Check yours in an online password checker. First, is it secure? Second, is it memorable?

## Quiz

Without reading the above section again or looking at any notes you've made, what is your password to the Statue of Liberty website? If you couldn't remember it, take a second to review the process. Do the activity. Picture the images. Add color, action, size, or touch. Figure out where you struggled.

## Exercise #4: Grocery Store Password

Imagine creating a password to login to the website of your favorite grocery store. Keep in mind that they have your credit card on file, so make sure you use unique images to make it more secure.

**A**: Picture the grocery store. When you think of it, what comes to mind? A specific section, the checkout lanes, the parking lot? Picture that in detail.

**F**: When you think of the store and the anchor, what does it remind you of? Picture this as the first link.

**S**: When you think of the first link, what comes to mind? Add this to the story or picture you're creating.

**T**: Relate the second link to something else, and picture that in the story.

**R**: Repeat; add another link. Or, **r**eview. Where can you add details? What can you make bigger, or sillier? Add action and turn the picture into a movie.

Mine: HANNOVERsnowANGELsoap

Hackable in around four quadrillion years, which I can live with.

See how the process works? We're not exactly creating a series of image, then trying to memorize them. The system is more about imagining the first item, which is naturally the catalyst or trigger for the next image. That image then reminds us of the next one, which reminds us of the next one, and so on.

This is the way your mind naturally works. You think of your best friend who loves movies, which reminds you of that time you had fun together, which brings to mind the movie you saw, and the lead actor's name. There's the password to the movie theater right there: BethphoenixthematrixKeanu.

Using this technique is working with the mind, not against it. Our minds are used to doing this. Your memory detective will be grateful.

# 9
# *The Phrase Chain Method*

## Method #2: The Phrase Chain Method in Action

I feel that the Word Chain Method, combined with your personal password system which we'll develop shortly, is easier to create, remember, and type. I'm including this system because for many people, a phrase comes to mind more easily than a series of words. They find it easier to create and easier to recall. If that's you, this method is perfect. Even if you were happy with how the Word Chain Method felt, read this section, do the exercises, and see if this is a better method for you.

Some security experts advocate using a method for password creation that may be more difficult to hack  than merely choosing three or four memorable words easily found in a dictionary. Instead of using words that trigger the memory of the next word, they recommend using a phrase that is easy for you to remember. You convert the long phrase into a abstract password by reducing it to the first letter of each word.

For example, a password for a travel website may be "AndMilesToGoBeforeISleep". While that is 24 characters, it's a well-known phrase filled with common words; it could be guessed if someone knows you like that phrase, or potentially figured out by a hacker using a brute force attack based on common phrases.

Converting the phrase to "Amtgbis" makes it harder to hack using a dictionary of common words or phrases. There are other issues with this specific example, though, which we'll cover below.

I find this this technique very helpful when a website allows only a small number of characters and requires the use of letters, numbers, and special characters. I created a password recently for a new website. The password was 26 characters, very easy for me to remember, and extremely difficult to hack. However, the website only allowed **22** characters, which messed everything up. Since I didn't want to have to remember that the password was the several words I combined, *minus* 4 characters, I had to redo the password.

For another website, they required a password up to 12 characters (not enough, in my opinion, for a strong password), and two or three words wouldn't have been secure enough. Using the Phrase Chain Method made it possible.

Let's see how we can use an easy-to-recall phrase but still create a secure password. While the last method wasn't "slower," it was AFSTR (a faster) way to remember passwords. With the Phrase Chain Method, you'll set A Personal Record (APR) when you create an **a**nchor, then a **p**hrase, and finally **r**eview.

### Exercise #5: Travel Website

Using the travel website example at the start of this section, we translate the phrase "And miles to go before I sleep" to: "Amtgbis". That is too short and very easy to hack (33% strength according to an online password checker).

Keeping nearly the same number of characters (which is my biggest concern, however), we could change it to "Am2gb4Is", but that only brings the strength up to 42%.

If a special character was required "Am2gb4!s" could be used, but due to its length this one could still be hacked in less than 60 seconds. It's easy to remember by connecting the anchor (travel website) with the thought of traveling, being tired, and still having miles to go before you sleep. Your personal password system, which we'll talk about shortly, could have every first letter capitalized, and every "I" could be a "!" instead.

But does it matter how easy it is to remember if it's not secure? No. How could we strengthen it? Adding characters would be great. Remember, a 12-character password is the recommended minimum length these days.

&m2gb4!sleepsnoredrool

This is much better, and no more difficult to remember. By combining the Word Chain Method with the Phrase Chain Method, we've created a password that is easy to remember and difficult to guess or hack. The only caution here is that making passwords easy to remember requires a system: your personal password system. If you are going to combine both methods, it's important to combine both methods every time, thus making it your personal system. You wouldn't want to use the Phrase Chain Method with three words at the end of the phrase only occasionally, because that's too hard to remember. "Did I add words at the end of this? I can't remember now." That's what you want to avoid. You'll be creating your personal system shortly, so you can just keep this in the back of your mind for now.

If your phrase is too short, you can use the first *two* letters of each word instead of adding words. Using our example above would give us "AnmitogobeIsl". This is considered fairly good, though still not very strong. Again, the key is the length. You could easily use the first three letters of each word, making it stronger but still easy to remember: "AndmiltogobeIsle".

For now, create your own password using this technique.

Step 1: Create your **a**nchor. What does the travel website remind you of? A far-off land? A sunny beach? Rome? The seven wonders of the world? Picture that.

Step 2: Think of a common saying or **p**hrase that relates to your anchor image. "When in Rome, do as the Romans do?" If nothing comes to mind, create your own saying. "I can't wait until I retire so I can travel the world!" "I'm going to see the seven wonders of the world before I die."

Step 3: Convert that phrase into a password of at least 12 characters. Use the first letter of each word, if your phrase is long enough. If it's not, use the first two letters of each word.

Step 4: **R**eview the anchor and phrase using CAS to add details.

You're still using the basic technique of thinking of the anchor and using what comes to mind (the cue or trigger) as the basis for creating and recalling the password.

## Exercise #6: Your Family's Website

Use this technique to create a password for your family's private website, a place where everyone can view pictures, leave messages, check on the home, etc. You need to secure it so no one has access.

Anchor: picture your family as a group, or everyone gathered around one computer, the name you create for your website, or a main value or idea of your family ("love" or "strong").

Think of a lengthly phrase that everyone will easily remember when shared with the family. Here are some ideas:

We're all one big happy family and we love each other no matter what.
"Waobhfawleonmw" is pretty good: 78% strength.

We're all crazy but we're our kind of crazy and I've got your back for ever.
"Wacbwokoc&igybfe" is better in part because of replacing "and" with "&".

We'll always be here for you John Boy, Elizabeth, and Mary Ellen our three angels.
"WabhfyJBE&ME03a" is great. It's a good length, uses numbers and letters, upper and lowercase letters, and a symbol. (I customized it with capitalization, numbers, and special characters. You don't have to do that yet. You'll learn how to add those shortly.)

Goodnight room, goodnight moon, goodnight cow jumping over the moon.
"Gnr,gnm,gncjotm" isn't bad, but could use a number and a special character to make it more secure.

Creating the phrase tends to be the most difficult part of this process. Try to describe who you are, your beliefs, what you want them to know, where you're located, or a favorite family saying. Here are two ideas that I could use for my family, which may spark your imagination:

We may be separated by many miles, but you all are always in my heart! (Wmbsbmm,by3aimh!)

I'm so thankful for the times we can spend together and wish we could do it more! (!mst4txwcst&wwcdim!)

Write down your phrase and translate it into a password. Aim for at least 12 characters. Review it once, and connect the image to your fictitious family website. Use CAST to add details: the faces of your family members around the table, a special family moment, or an unforgettable holiday. Cement the saying or expression into your mind.

Look at mine and consider yours:
Memorable? Check.
Secure? Check.
Excessive? Possibly.

Each of us has to decide the level of security we're comfortable with. Most everyone is happy with a simple password until something bad happens. When their social media account is hacked, or their email account is hijacked and used to send spam to everyone they know, it's embarrassing. It can be time consuming and difficult to get the account back under control. If you're a public figure, respected member of the community, or have an important job, it can be extra problematic.

Recently a friend's social media account was hacked. The hacker immediately changed the email address associated with the account and the password, locking my friend out. In fact, my friend didn't find out about it until I sent him a text saying, "Are we chatting on social media right now? It doesn't sound like you." He replied that we weren't chatting. He checked and couldn't even login to his account. A week later he still didn't have control, even after much effort.

While the type of security above (Wacbwokoc&!gyb4e) for a simple family website may seem too much, consider your private information becoming public: the family discussion about the annoying neighbor, or how long the house will be empty when you're on vacation.

It's similar to locking the door of your home. Some people never lock their doors, while some are perfectly happy with a cheap lock. Others have an armed-response security company monitoring the home 24/7. Upgrade your cybersecurity to at least equal your home security.

## Quiz

Close your eyes and recall the password to your family's website.

Can you still recall your password for the Statue of Liberty website?

How about your grocery store website password?

Compare the ease of the Word Chain Method to the Phrase Chain Method. Which system do you find easier for creating a password? Which can you recall better? Which do you feel is more secure? Experiment and choose the one that works best for you, then pick one and stick with it. You'll customize it in the next section as you create your personal password system.

# 10
# *Your Personal Password System*

The Word Chain or Phrase Chain Methods may seem plenty secure, but they need some slight refinement. You must create your own password system to make the process complete. More and more websites require passwords with uppercase and lowercase letters, special characters, and one or more numbers. Creating an entirely unique password for each website, with random capitalization, number, and special character replacement, undoubtedly adds to the level of security. It also makes the passwords harder to remember. "Hmm, the Statue of Liberty website. Did I capitalize the first letter of each word, or the second? Or maybe this site had the first word capitalized. Wait, maybe I used the Phrase Chain for this one..." That doesn't serve us. We want to have secure passwords that are easy to remember. We want our lives to be easier, not harder.

The solution is your own system. If you decided that the Word Chain Method is best for you, use that. Maybe you always capitalize the last letter in your password, or the first complete word. There are many options, and you'll use this chapter to create your own system.

You may be tempted to write your system down, but I don't recommend it. Use your memory. Since you're creating the system, it should be easy to remember. If you must write it down, put it on paper and place it in a locked safe.

## The System

### Part 1 of 4: Word Chain, Phrase Chain, or Combination

The first part of your system involves choosing which method you prefer. Make your choice and stick with it. The Word Chain method tends to be easier to type on a keyboard. Many people find the Phrase Chain to be easier on a smart phone or tablet, as it tends to produce shorter passwords (don't forget: 12 character minimum for either method).

### Exercise #7: Your Preferred Method

Decide now which method you prefer: the Word Chain Method or Phrase Chain Method.

### Part 2 of 4: Capitalization System

Using both uppercase and lowercase letters makes your password harder to guess or hack, adding security without making it harder to remember... as long as you keep track of which letters are capitalized. Create your own system so you always capitalize using the same method. Here are some examples, using a variety of Word Chain and Phrase Chain methods, including combinations:

- ALWAYS capitalize the first real word.
1028oBIGappleiicmitimia! ("If I can make it there I'll make it anywhere!")

- Always Capitalize The First Letter Of Any Word.
  GreenwichVillageWashingtonSquareParkNyu

- aLways cApitalize tHe sEcond lEtter oF aNy wOrd.
  "Much harder to type, but much less obvious than above" gives us "mHtT,bMlOtA".

- alwayS capitalizE thE lasT letteR oF eacH worD.
  geTsavErecalLpicturEconnecTrevieW

Capitalizing every other letter, or every third, etc. is much easier with the Phrase Chain Method than the Word Chain Method. Plus, as you create your system, keep in mind on which device you type most of your passwords. Using the shift key to capitalize many letters can be annoyingly time consuming on tablets and smart phones.

### Exercise #8: Your Preferred Capitalization System
Decide now which capitalization method you will use.

### Part 3 of 4: Special Character Substitution System

Most websites require at least one special character, which may be difficult to remember. How can we add the special character the website requires without making our lives more difficult and overworking our memory? Substituting a special character for a letter or number that's already in the password we created makes it much easier. We don't necessarily want to randomly add a special character to the password we create, because it's easy to forget that this password ends with an exclamation point. Plus, this is what most people do. "Oh, I need a special character for this site. Well, I'll use my cat's name, my favorite number, and end it with '!'. Done." It's too easy to hack.

To substitute letters for characters, some easily come to mind: "S" = "$", "1" = "!", or "A" = "@". Unfortunately, hackers are aware of these and already have methods to overcome them. To stay ahead, you need to create your own system. You can create a substitution based on what the character and/or letter remind you of. In addition to the chart in the previous chapter, here are some ideas:

- X = + (+ on its side looks like X)
- P = + (P for plus, + is the plus symbol)
- R = ? (R for The Riddler, ? for the symbol on his outfit)
- H = ^ (H for House, ^ for roof of house)
- S = * (* looks like a snowflake)

I believe the best idea is to *randomly* assign a special character to a letter. Don't use "1" = "!", "2" = "@", "3" = "#", etc. That's too common and too easy to hack. Pick a common letter like "A" or "I". Randomly pick a special character that is easy to find on your keyboard and phone. Create a link in your mind between the two, using Picture, Connect, Review. "I" = ")" because you're always happy and ")" is the smile in an emoticon. "I" = "#1" because "I am number one!"

## Exercise #9: Special Character(s) Substitutions

Decide which special character(s) you will substitute for which letters.

Feeling overwhelmed? Don't worry, we'll practice putting it all together as soon as we get through one more system.

Mentally review your system so far.
Which password creation method do you prefer?
Which words or letters will you always capitalize?

Which special character(s) will you use, and what letter(s) will they replace?

### Part 4 of 4: Number Substitution System

The last part is a variation of the special character substitution. By changing a letter with a number, we automatically add numbers to our passwords. This keeps us from the too-common and easily hacked method of adding a two-digit number to the end of our password.

Again, we need to **avoid the obvious: a straight-up substitution of A=1, B=2, C=3, etc.** You'll invent your own system that isn't based on an idea others might come up with. Instead, change every "A" to "8" or "7." Why? For absolutely no reason. It's completely random. Every "E" could be "4" or change "D" to "1".

More and more websites require two numbers. To make our lives easier, let's create a system that takes this into account. "A" = "87", for example. To plan for the future when websites require three digits, or make it more difficult to hack shorter passwords, "A" could be "493", for example. Create this substitution using a reason that makes sense to you alone. Avoid using your postal (zip) code, your house or apartment number, date of birth, or any other number that can be easily associated with you. Also avoid common favorite numbers such as 21, 64, 69 or 420, and the current year. Four years from now it will be difficult to remember that this was the year you created the password. Trust me, I learned that one the hard way.

Now, for your personal system, pick two or three frequently used letters and translate them to one or two digit numbers. Here are a few recommendations:

- Use a frequently used, common letter such as "E", "T", or "A".
- If you only choose to replace one letter, replace it with at least two digits: "E" = "47", for example.
- If you can replace more than one letter with a number, one digit is good, but two is better. "T" = "7" and ""A" = "3" is fine, for example, but "E" = "47" and "T" = "76" is better.
- Replace the first letter of your partner's or best friend's name with his or her favorite number.
- Replace the letter "S" with the year you went skydiving, or the letter "T" with your personal best race time.

## Exercise #10: Number Substitutions
Decide which digit(s) will replace which letter(s).

## Review

Cement your new system in your memory by reviewing it now.

Which password creation method do you prefer?
Which words or letters will you always capitalize?
Which special character(s) will you use, and what letter(s) will they replace?
Which number(s) replace which letter(s)?

## Examples

Using the character and number substitutions will dramatically increase your password security level. We create a memorable password using linked words or a phrase that gets translated into a shorter chain. We then substitute our pre-selected characters and numbers for the appropriate letters, creating even more secure passwords and satisfying the requirements of the websites.

Let's see this in action. Do you remember our example for the Statue of Liberty website password? One of them was:
AppleWormFishingThisBig!

A minor issue with this password is that it has no numbers and only one special character. A bigger issue is that the special character is at the end, which is where everyone dumps the required character. While this password is certainly secure enough for us to use for the Statue of Liberty website, keep in mind that our overall goal is to create a system so we can easily and quickly create memorable passwords. **It's easier to have one system that you use everywhere, even if it is excessive for some websites.**

What if every "A" is a number instead, like above?
87ppleWormFishingThisBig!

Combining the special character and number substitutions, with "I" = "#1":
87ppleWormF#1sh#1ngTh#1sB#1g!

That's 29 characters, and seems excessive. It could be safely shortened to:
87ppleWormF#1sh#1ng
Even "87ppleWormF#1sh" is fine with a 99% strength rating.

How much effort you put into your personal system is up to you. It also depends a great deal on how secure you need your passwords to be. You've seen in this book that even the most difficult looking passwords can be easy to remember. You've also seen that the most difficult to remember passwords can be easy to hack.

In creating a password for your online bank account with the Phrase Chain Method, first you select the anchor: the bank, which reminds me of money. Money reminds me of: You Never Give Me Your Money/Can't Buy Me Love/The Best Things In Life Are Free. I've substituted "01" for "B" and "?" for "R" and capitalized the first letters of the first phrase.

YNGMYMco1mltbtil?f

Using the Word Chain Method, the anchor is still the bank, which reminds me of money. Money reminds me of "ka-ching", replacing "A" with "493" and "I" with ")". "Ka" sounds like "car" and reminded me of my Prius, again replacing "I" with ")". Since it's nearly time to get a new car, I'm reminded that I have to Save for it, replacing "A" with "493" again.
K493-ch)ngPr)usS493ve

The passwords I create should make sense to you, but not necessarily be easy for you to remember. That's understandable: you didn't create them. Your brain doesn't fire the same way mine does. Perhaps you're not a Beatles fan and would never have thought of those songs in relation to money. Or you've never used the word "Ka-ching" in your life. No problem! The beauty of this concept is that your mind and memory create the connections, and your mind has created the substitution systems. Your overall personal password system makes *your* passwords easy for *you* to remember, but incredibly hard to hack.

Looking at the above examples, you may wonder: do I really use, and recommend, a 22-character password? Yes. Why not? With the Word Chain Method especially, a 20-30 character password is easy to remember and type. If that seems impractical to you, consider how easy it is to recall bank password above. It requires only:

- Three links: "Ka-ching", "Prius", and "Save".
- The capitalization system is the first letter of each word, which is simple to remember.
- The special character substitution is ")" for any "I", which is also easy.
- Finally, the number replacement is "493", a randomly created number but easy for me to remember as part of my overall system.

This is an extremely secure password that is easy to remember, proving that security is easier than we think. In the real world, you may be content with:

K493-ch)ngS493ve

This shorter version is still considered excellent, with a strength rating of 100%. It's slightly easier to type and, with 16 characters, is still robust.

You're about to create new passwords and update old less secure ones using your system. Don't worry if this seems difficult. Your system will get easier to use and recall over time, and it will feel natural very soon. Using these methods enhances your creativity, sharpens your memory, and strengthens your cybersecurity all at the same time.

Now it's time to put all you've learned into use.

# 11

# *Practicing Your New Skills*

## Review

To practice your entire personal password system, do a quick review. Mentally list each of your systems.

1. Password creation method:
2. Capitalization system:
3. Special character system:
4. Number replacement system:

Let's create several new passwords using your new system. Before letting ourselves loose on the real world, we'll practice with made up websites.

## Exercise #11: Social Media Website

*Yearly*: A New Social Media Website

You've been invited to join *Yearly*, the exclusive, niche social media website for people born the same year as you.

Anchor: decide what *Yearly* reminds you of. You could also choose what happened the year you were born, your parents, the hospital or town you were born in, or anything else that comes to mind when you think of this website, group, or idea. What comes to mind when you think of *Yearly*?

Word Chain Method:
- **F**irst link: take the anchor and associate it with something else that it reminds you of.
- **S**econd link: what does the first link remind you of?
- **T**hird link: what does the second link remind you of?
- **R**eview all the images and add detail using CAST.

Phrase Chain Method:
- What **p**hrase is associated with the anchor? Translate the phrase into the password.
- **R**eview.

Take a moment to complete this exercise. It's okay if you're finding it difficult. Learning any new skill can be challenging, and mental skills are no different (they're possibly even harder). It can be especially tough if we're not used to being creative. Do your best. Below are some ideas if you're completely stuck. I'll offer fewer and fewer hints as we transition through the exercises. I've gotten feedback that half the fun of taking my password seminar is hearing the wild ideas I use as examples, but soon you'll be creating those fun images all on your own.

*Yearly* anchor ideas (general first, then specific to me):
Old
Long ago in a galaxy far, far away
Aching back
Knees
Finally a Facebook replacement
Gold (exclusive)
New Year's Eve
Baby New Year
Father Time

Should old acquaintance be forgot and never brought to mind
Moon landing
South Dakota

Let's take one and expand on it.

Word Chain Method
Anchor: gold
First link: chain
Second link: tow
Third link: stuck
Review: using a solid gold chain to tow a stuck blue pickup truck out of the mud.

Phrase Chain Method
Anchor: gold
Phrase: all that glitters is not gold
Review: using a fingernail to scrape at the gold chain, see the flakes drop away while realizing that it's not a solid gold chain...all that glitters is not gold.

Next, create the actual password from the images. Use your capitalization, special character, and number systems. Write it down so you can see it in action.

Word Chain Example
"ChainTowStuck" is a starting point. Using some ideas from the previous chapter, we change it to:
Ch493)nTowStuck

Phrase Chain Example
"AlThGlIsNoGo" is a starting point. "493lThGl)sNoGo" is what it gets changed to after adding the character and number

systems. Interestingly, using merely one capital letter reduces the strength only slightly. If you're creating passwords and you enter them frequently on a phone or tablet, be aware that including at least one capital letter is important, but you don't have to make your life difficult by overdoing it.

Both of these have "Excellent" security levels and will satisfy the requirements of most websites for secure passwords.

A note about imagination: anything that pops into your head is correct. A friend read an early draft of this section and had a question. Every time she saw the word *Yearly* she thought of "yearling" — a young horse. She created a great password based on yearling but was worried she was doing it wrong. No! As long as you're consistent in your thinking, whatever you create as an anchor and links is fine. Since she thought of a young horse every time she tried to create a password for *Yearly*, she would probably think the same way the next time she goes back to the website. It would trigger the same thought process, and bring her back to her memorable, secure password based on horses (instead of the year she was born), so there would be no problem at all.

### Exercise #12: Test Your Passwords Online

Now is the time to go to an online password checking website and test your creations. **Don't wait until you create passwords for real sites.** Entering a actual password into a checking site is not recommended.

### Exercise #13: Shopping Website

*SuperCheapo*: A New Site for Daily Deep Discounts

Time to shop. Register for this new website for deep

discounts. This website will have your credit card on file. Does that matter? No, because all your passwords are already very secure using your personal password system. Keep in mind that creating secure passwords can be a playful experience. Use your creativity and imagination to make yourself smile as you do the exercise.

**A**nchor: What does *SuperCheapo* remind you of? Do you have a friend who is notoriously cheap? When you think of online shopping, does something come immediately to mind? Does the idea of saving money trigger a memory? Create an image to use as your anchor.

Word Chain Method:
- ○ **F**irst link: take the anchor and associate it with something else that it reminds you of.
- ○ **S**econd link: what does the first link remind you of?
- ○ **T**hird link: what does the second link remind you of?
- ○ **R**eview all the images and add detail using CAST.

Phrase Chain Method:
- ○ **P**hrase: what comes to mind in association with the anchor?
- ○ **R**eview the phrase and add details about how it connects to the anchor.

Using your capitalization, special character, and number systems, write out the password. If needed, add the extra step of writing it out plainly first, then adding the systems.

Word Chain Example
Anchor/Links: "deal" reminds me of *Deal or No Deal*,

which reminds me of Howie Mandel, which reminds me of bald, which reminds me of my friend Barry.

HowieBaldBarry = How)eB493ldB493rry

Phrase Chain Example

Anchor/Phrase: "deal" which reminds me of *Deal or No Deal*.

"DeorNoDe". Here we have a problem. It's too short; there are no special characters and no "I" or "A" for me to replace with my numbers. What now? I could add "E" to my letter system, which might complicate things later on when I try to remember if a password was created before or after I added "E" as a replaced letter.

There is still time to change your system if you notice limitations. If you choose to modify your system, you can do it now by adding another letter that you replace with a number. It's probably easier, though, to think of a different phrase instead of changing your system.

Let's try a phrase from an old movie: "I'll buy that for a dollar!" "Ilbuthfoado" becomes ")lbuthfo493do".

Surprisingly, this registers as only 77% strength and ranks as "Fairly Good." Is that good enough for a site with your credit card? For me, that's too weak.

Maybe a reminder not to buy too much on the *SuperCheapo* site: "It's not how much you make, it's how much you keep."

)Tnohomuyoma,)thomuyoke

It's often difficult for me to create a long memorable phrase. I recommend the Word Chain Method if possible. It tends to be easier to create, remember, and type, and rarely is it a problem to create passwords with enough characters to be secure. (The opposite happens occasionally when a website won't allow an easy-to-remember, easy-to-type 26 character password.)

How does this feel so far? It might not feel easy yet, but believe me, that feeling is right around the corner.

Are you ready to update actual, real-world passwords? I want you to be comfortable with these before you commit to your actual passwords. I don't want you to excitedly replace a password, only to forget it next week and feel discouraged when you have to click on the "Forgot password" button.

If you're not feeling comfortable yet, create a password for *LOUD!*, a new music streaming website featuring only music designed to be played loud. Try one for *Will It Rain On Your Head*, a weather app that uses your exact GPS coordinates to predict the weather right above you. Finally, what would be a secure password for *Flatten*, a website for ironing enthusiasts?

## Quiz

Without reviewing your notes, what is your password for *Yearly*? What is the password for *SuperCheapo*?

Review your systems one final time.
1. Password creation method:
2. Capitalization system:
3. Special character system:
4. Number replacement system:

# 12

# *The Assigned Password System*

For extra security, there are many companies and some websites that require the use of a randomly generated password supplied to you. How are you supposed to remember these? Most people write the password down and keep it near the computer, which is fine from an online security standpoint, but bad for security locally. To remember it instead, we'll use the same basic technique as you've already learned, along with a few special pre-memorized systems to make it easier and (somewhat) palatable.

## Time Investment

Assigned passwords are slightly more difficult to recall than the ones you create yourself, but remembering them can be done. This is an even bigger learning curve. Is it worth the time to learn to memorize the passwords you're given? Yes. If you are accessing sites that require this level of security, I doubt the people running it would be happy knowing you've written the assigned password on a sticky note and "hidden" it in your desk drawer, wallet, or purse. You have no choice, so use this system to make it as painless as possible.

**This section may be skimmed or skipped if you never receive assigned passwords that can't be changed to a different secure password using your personal**

**password system from the previous chapter.**

## Are They Secure?

The real question here is: do they work? Are those weird passwords filled with strange characters any harder to hack than ones you create yourself? We know they are harder to remember, but are they more effective?

As long as the password is entirely random, unique, and not based on a rule, it can be more secure than the Word Chain or Phrase Chain Methods. Let's assume that whoever is assigning you a password knows what they are doing. If you're doing this on your own, through a random password generating website or other means, keep in mind that the recommended minimum length is still 12 characters! Just because a password *looks* hard to hack doesn't mean it is. *Don't equate "hard to remember" with "hard to hack!"*

Here's an example. This password was created by an internet-based random password generator that allowed me to designate the number of characters:
5B18m\

Seems like it would be hard to break, right?

Evaluation:
- Potentially difficult to remember, though pretty easy when you finish reading this chapter. (Five giant bumble bees attack an 18-wheel tractor trailer, driven by a small monkey, who uses the emergency escape slide to get away.)
- Low strength.
- Too short: only six characters.

- A standard desktop PC could hack this in about two hours. A medium-size botnet could hack it in less than a second.
- Overall, it's horrible. Hard for most people to remember, but easy to hack.

Here's a good one that a random password generator created:

37q9F79*zzb&CJ&c

Evaluation:
- 100% strength.
- 16 characters long is great.
- 143 billion years to hack.

The problem: how long would this take you to memorize? What we need is a system. We perform a little upfront work to make it much easier in the long run to memorize the passwords and update them as needed. This system has a few components: one each to cover the letters, numbers, and special characters that these random passwords contain.

You can put effort into this now and customize each component, or keep this book handy as a reference. Whenever you get a password to memorize, just refer to each of the following sections to translate your password into something you can remember. It's like having a code book that you use to decrypt the code. Having the code book accessible to use when you need to change your creative images back into a password is much safer than having the unencrypted password written on a piece of paper.

**The Alphabet Images**

When you receive a password like "m8L-fsC%9zw6" you

need a way to picture each part so you can create an interesting, memorable story. The first system is a way to easily translate letters into memorable images.

You need at least one clear image for each letter of the alphabet. Here are some suggestions. Pick one that jumps out to you, or use your own. Which do you prefer: an object, a character (like Zorro), or an action? Ask yourself, "What does the letter 'A' remind me of? An apple, or an alien?" Don't get too set on your choice, as next you'll be looking at capitalization and numbers. Avoid duplication. You don't want to think of "ant" as both "A" and the number 6 (ants have six legs).

| Letter | Images | Your Image | Letter | Images | Your Image |
|--------|--------|-----------|--------|--------|-----------|
| A | Apple; alien; android | | N | Nachos; nut; nurse | |
| B | Banana; bee; baby | | O | Orange; ostrich; owl | |
| C | Cookie; cow; computer | | P | Puppy; pizza; pineapple | |
| D | Dad; duck; donut | | Q | Quiche; queen | |
| E | Elephant; egg; eagle | | R | Rhinoceros; rabbit | |
| F | French fries; flamingo | | S | Squirrel; snail; soda | |
| G | Giraffe; grapes | | T | Tiger; taco; toast | |
| H | Hamburger; hotel | | U | Umbrella; unicorn | |
| I | Igloo; iguana; ice cream | | V | Vampire; van | |
| J | Juice box; jaguar; jump rope | | W | Whale; waffles; watermelon | |
| K | King Kong; knife; kiwi | | X | X-ray; xylophone | |
| L | Lobster; lemon; lasagna | | Y | Yo-yo; yak; yacht | |
| M | Marshmallow; muffin | | Z | Zorro; zebra | |

## Capital Letters

For capital letters, there are a few choices. One is to make the image for a capital letter *huge* when you translate the password into a series of images. This works for some, but others rely on making images extra-large as part of the CAST process. "m8L-fsC%9zw6" becomes a regular size **m**uffin but a huge **l**obster.

To make it easier in the long run, assign two different images to each letter. One image above is for the lowercase letter, one is for the uppercase letter. "m8L-fsC%9zw6" has a regular size **m**uffin instead of a **m**arshmallow, and a **l**emon instead of a **l**obster. Make sure you write down which is which as you create the system, even if you choose not to memorize it.

## Images for Numbers

We also need to quickly and easily translate numbers into pictures. Here are a few ideas based on what the number either looks like or reminds me of. Pick one or write down your own. If you're creating your own, make sure that you don't use the same image twice (the image of a donut for both "D" and zero, for example).

| Number | Images | Your Image |
|--------|--------|-----------|
| 0 | Soccer ball; frisbee | |
| 1 | Baseball bat; candle; flag pole with flag | |
| 2 | Shoes; twins | |
| 3 | Tricycle; 3-ring circus; little pigs | |
| 4 | Chair; car; playing card (4 suits) | |
| 5 | Fingers; 5 looks like a fish hook | |
| 6 | Ant; six-pack | |
| 7 | 7 looks like a boomerang, boomerang = kangaroo; swan (7 swans a'swimming) | |
| 8 | Octopus; spider | |
| 9 | Cat (nine lives); 9 looks like lasso | |

# Images for Special Characters

Special characters play a big part in the randomized, assigned passwords. Here's a sample system for for characters.

| Character | Images | Your Image |
|---|---|---|
| ~ | Ocean wave; surfboard | |
| ! | Rocket ship; pogo stick | |
| @ | Car doing 'donuts'; spinning top | |
| # | Hopscotch, tic-tac-toe; very difficult football goalpost | |
| $ | Money; dollar bill | |
| % | See-saw/teeter-totter; skateboard | |
| ^ | Pyramid; roof of house; teepee | |
| & | Snake; merry-go-round | |
| * | Star (on door, in sky, or favorite movie star) | |
| ( | Sad clown; eyebrow | |
| ) | Happy person; door handle | |
| – | Tight rope; tug of war | |
| + | Calculator; wedding ("+1") | |
| \ | Slide; leaning tower of Pisa | |
| < | Pac Man; shark | |
| > | Pinocchio; bird | |
| , | Banana peel; snail | |
| . | Rock; basketball | |
| = | Train; Grand Canyon | |

I know this can seem daunting. There is a lot to learn and remember before you start memorizing passwords. Keep in mind the learning curve example earlier. We learn to drive not because it's easy to learn, but because it will be much more convenient and faster in the future. The time invested is worth it in the long run.

I've found that the easiest way to approach this is to take it one password at a time. Receive your assigned password and pull out this book. Use a piece of paper to write out the images needed, then combine them to make a memorable story. Use the "3x" rule and you're on your way. Repeat the next time you have a tough password, and over time you'll commit the charts to memory by using them. (Properly discard the paper with the translated images when you've successfully memorized the password.)

**The Story Chain Method**

Here are the steps. Review these, then we'll work through them with an example below.

Step 1: Picture the anchor. As with the Word and Phrase Chain Methods, you *must* start with the anchor. This is where people often have trouble. They get so focused on memorizing the password that they forget to connect to the system it is needed for.

Step 2: Take the assigned password and translate each character into the image. Most people write down the associated images first, without trying to create a scenario for them. It's easier for some people to think of the scenario as they go. Use whichever is better for you.

Step 3: Picture the anchor and the first link. Create a story around them.

Step 4: Continue with each link, adding to the story with each word. This now becomes the Word Chain Method. It's slightly more difficult because you must create a story based on a provided word, instead of asking yourself what else the link reminds you of, and creating the next link image on your own.

Step 5: Starting with the anchor, review the entire story three to five times, adding details with CAST. See the story in your mind.

If you struggle to create a story and link each image in the chain together, pretend you're telling a story to a child. The child has given you a few ideas about what she wants to hear about for her bedtime story. It's your job to make something up for her.

**Example**

Here's an example for us to do together before you try one mostly on your own. This is a randomly generated password:
37q9F79*zzb&

1. Anchor: let's say this password is for logging in to your work at the wind turbine factory. Picture the factory or a huge wind turbine.
2. Translate each character. Refer to the charts or make up your own: tricycle, boomerang, queen, cat, flamingo, boomerang, cat, star, *two* zebras, bee, snake
3. Imagine the anchor and the first link together. Create a story. Set aside your grownup self and just play. Picture the wind turbine soaring above a children's playground. A child rides a **tricycle** in circles around the base of the wind turbine.
4. Continue linking images by adding to your story. Then she runs over a **boomerang**, breaking it in half. The child continues riding, crashing into the **queen**, who is holding her **cat**. The cat jumps down to chase a huge **flamingo** that has in its mouth a different **cat** with a clear white **star** on its coat. Nearby, *two* **zebras** carefully lead a **bee** away from a coiled, angry snake.
5. Review the story, adding details. What color is the tricycle? How old is the queen? What happens to the cat in the mouth of the flamingo?

Picture this scene three to five times, adding details each

time, and you will have it. This process may take a few minutes, but imagine how much more secure your password is in your mind instead of writing it down. Think of how impressed people will be that you committed to memory such a seemingly difficult-to-remember password. Your IT department will be grateful that you're doing a great job keeping everything secure.

**Exercise #14: Your New Job**

Congratulations. You've been accepted to the position of bank president for Too Big to Fail Bank and Trust. The IT department has provided you with your new password. Even though you are the president, there's no way to change it to make it easier to remember. You have to use it to unlock your computer every time you leave and return to your desk. You decide that you'll use the Assigned Password System to quickly memorize it.

Your new password is:

3F*d2Uz4w9u%UJ

1. Anchor. Imagine Too Big to Fail Bank and Trust, being president of the bank, your corner office, huge desk, or lots and lots of money.
2. Translate each character.

tricycle, French fries, star, duck, shoes, Umbrella, zebra, chair, watermelon, cat, unicorn, teeter-totter (see-saw), Umbrella, Juice box. (Note how we replace the capital letters based on the appropriate image from the chart.)

3. Imagine the anchor and link number one. Can you imagine a bank vault with a child riding a tricycle inside?
4. Link more images. Do this part on your own.
5. Review.

**Don't continue until you've completed the exercise.** If you have trouble, or it seems daunting, use the technique of telling a child a story using the words she gave you. Make it fun.

Here's the story I created to tell my niece. "Once upon a time there was a huge bank with lots and lots of money. One day a little girl — just like you — snuck into the vault, which is a safe room where they store all the money. She knew she wasn't supposed to be playing there, but besides the money, there was a lot of other fun stuff inside.

First she rode the tricycle that was there, and ate all the French fries in a giant box. She got so full she fell down and hit her head — she saw stars all around her, just like in the cartoons. A duck wearing high heel shoes and carrying an umbrella jumped on top of a zebra, who walked over and tried to sit on a chair next to the little girl. The chair collapsed under the weight of the zebra and duck, and the zebra fell down and landed on a watermelon on the floor, squishing it.

The zebra fed a piece of the watermelon to the little girl's cat, while they all watched a unicorn run back and forth on a see-saw, first one side went down, then the other. Attached to the unicorn's horn was a giant umbrella, because it was raining juice from a juice box the little girl was squeezing. What a fun vault to be in!"

Memorizing anything is possible with a system and an active imagination!

## Memory Palace Method

There are times when creating a long story by linking all the words together is too difficult. It would be easier — and make more sense — to split the story up into several pieces. There is a way to do this, which may make memorizing a provided 16-character secure password easier.

You may have heard of the method of loci, or the concept of a memory palace. This technique has you connecting your images to a *location*, instead of to each other in a long chain. You create a short story or image, connect that to a location or object you can easily visualize, then repeat.

**Exercise #15: Create a Memory Palace**

To create a memory palace, most people use their office, kitchen, bedroom, or entire home. You could also use the route to work or home, your favorite grocery store, or shopping mall.

Let's start with your home. Imagine standing in the doorway to your favorite room. Look to the left and identify what's there. Is it a wall or a corner? Either way, what is interesting about it? Is there a couch along the wall? Is there a lamp in the corner? That's location number one in your memory palace.

Next, continue around the room clockwise. What is the next obvious feature of the room? Most likely, it's either a corner or a wall, and that location has something in it: furniture, a television, a framed photo or painting, etc. If you're in the kitchen, it might be the toaster first, then the sink, then the counter, then the refrigerator, and so on.

Mentally walk through the room and pick the first eight most obvious places (locations nine and ten will be the ceiling and the middle of the floor). For most rooms, that will be:

   1. wall (couch, TV, photo, desk)
   2. corner (lamp, plant)
   3. wall - main feature

4. corner - main feature
5. wall - main feature
6. corner - main feature
7. wall - main feature
8. corner - main feature
9. ceiling (fan, light figure, painted ceiling)
10. middle of the floor (carpet, rug, tile, etc.)

Any room should provide ten locations to store images.

Use the same technique to create a memory journey. Think of your favorite shopping mall, or the path you take to work or school. Identify 10 or 20 obvious locations along the route that you would think of easily next time you mentally walk the path. That's another 10-20 places to store information.

## Exercise #16: Your New Home Security System (Memory Palace Method)

You're very security conscious, so you've installed a keyboard on the door to your home. You now need to enter a 20-character password to get inside:
@Rkvb%+^a63rp8=$SW@B

You know the process. This time, instead of creating one very long story image, you'll split up the password into reasonable segments.
1. Anchor: your home. Use the room you chose above.
2. Translate.
Car doing "donuts", Rhino, kite, vampire, banana... (Fill in the rest yourself.)
3. Imagine. Picture your first location in your home memory palace. Imagine a car — just big enough for you to fit inside, doing donuts in that space. If it's too small of a

space for that, picture a child with a toy car covered in ink doing donuts with the car on the wall, piece of furniture, or whatever is there, ruining it. Imagine a large rhinoceros running towards the car and ramming it with its horn, still in your first location.

4. Link. Next, move to the second location. See it in your mind. Imagine flying a kite in that space, then add the vampire to the picture. Is the vampire flying the kite? Be careful. Don't mix up the order. Maybe the kite is flying the vampire? Perhaps the vampire swoops in and tells you not to fly the kite in the house, especially so close to that item in the corner or along the wall. In your mind, move to the third location. Picture the banana on a see-saw. Continue around the room, filling in each location with the images you see from my chart or ones you've created yourself.

5. Review. Mentally review your room, starting from the first location. See what's in each spot, adding detail as you go. I find it's very effective to think of scenarios where my stuff will get damaged. That's easy for me to remember.

For long passwords, I prefer the Memory Palace Method. I find it easier to connect a few items to one location, then move on to the next. You can place only one object image per location, but if you have a longer password to remember, use two or even three images per location.

Now you know how to memorize even the longest, toughest looking passwords. It takes a few, but the rewards last for as long as you need to enter that password. It also gets easier and faster as you practice.

# Part 3:

# Passwords in the

# Real World

# 13
# *Upgrading Your Cyber Security*

You've created systems, exercised your mind, and improved both your creativity and memory abilities. Now it's time to replace those old passwords with new, more secure ones. Before you start, however, it's important to learn the most common problem areas, so you can be sure to avoid them.

## Common Problems

1. **Weak anchor.** It's difficult to recall a word or phrase chain if the anchor isn't vivid enough. You must find a strong initial anchor image. For example, when I first started developing this system, I created a password for my bank. The anchor was, obviously, the bank. The problem: it was too vague, and I had trouble recalling the first link in the word chain. The connection of the images wasn't clear enough. Eventually I switched to a more specific anchor, using a particular feature of the bank that always caught my eye. I created a new password that used that feature as the anchor and first link, and had no problems after that. If you're struggling to recall a password, give extra thought to the anchor image.

2. **Overly complex system.** If you were a bit overzealous

in the creation of your capitalization, special character, or number replacement systems, you may be struggling. "Which letter did I capitalize? Did I substitute a '^' for an 'H' or not?" Review your system to make sure it's set in your mind. If it's too complex, simplify your system, especially the capitalization system. Capitalize the second or third letter, the last letter, or the first and last. Check your password strength. More than likely, one or two capital letters are fine. More than that doesn't add much — if anything — to the strength of your password.

3. **Typing issues.** There have been plenty of times when I've felt like I've forgotten a password, only to realize that it's a typing issue. It's easy to accidentally type "o" instead of ")". If you have trouble with a password, try typing it very slowly. Turn on the "Show Password" feature if it's available, so you can double check it before hitting "Enter." If you login with it a few times and always have trouble, you may need to create a different one.

4. **Infrequent use.** It's now getting easier to create and remember passwords using your personal password system... at least for a few days. The trouble comes when you sign up for a website, create your secure, easy-to-recall password, then not use the site again for weeks, months, or years. One day, you need to get back into your account. You bought holiday presents in November, then the following year decide to use the same shopping site again — but what is that password? It's been a year. Are you really expected to remember it? Yes, you can. If you created a clear anchor and first link, the rest should fall into place. If not, it won't pop into your mind. For this issue, it's worth adding a lot of detail to your passwords, especially the anchor and first link, or anchor and phrase.

Think it through. Add action. Imagine it in your mind as bigger, uglier, fancier, smellier. Think of a horrible color combination. Periodically review your passwords. I don't suggest writing out your passwords unless you can store them in a locked location, preferably away from your computer area. You may consider, however, listing the names of the websites you have created passwords for. This has a small inherent risk associated with it. It's a road map to anyone who wants to hack you specifically. They could look at your list and start using what they know about you to attempt to break into your websites. They'd have all the help they need with your complete list. If infrequent use is a big problem, consider writing down the websites you sign up for. Then, weekly or monthly, test yourself. Look at the company name where you bought the holiday presents and think, "Yes, those were great presents. It's been a month, what was that password? Oh yes, the anchor was the image of the bullseye, and the first link was 'Arrow'. That brought to mind 'Robin Hood' and 'tights'. ArrowRobinHoodTights becomes '493rrowRob)nHoodT)ghts'. That was easy."

5. **A lack of creativity.** As adults, we tend to be (or try to be) serious and mature. Memory works best with unique, creative, odd, strange images. If you see a dog out for a walk, that's not very memorable. If you see a *huge* dog out for a walk, with purple fur, six legs, four ears, and huge, gleaming, sharp teeth, you're going to remember it (and tell others about it, making the memory even stronger). Don't think: "The anchor for the store with the holiday presents is a bullseye, then I think of an arrow, then Robin Hood, then tights, okay, got it." Think: "Bullseye, it's red and white and I see it on their signs, semi trailers, and the store front. I can picture it. I wonder why they didn't put

an arrow into the logo. I can just imagine a huge, 3D arrow sticking out of the center of it. The arrow itself is green — the green and red will remind me of the holiday. Who shoots the arrow? Robin Hood. Oh, I can picture him easily. Ugh, those green tights. Imagine if green tights for men became the fashion statement this year! And the store would sell them, and those funny hats, too. I could buy them for Dad — well, at least the hat. He'd never wear the tights, no matter how popular they are. Dad in green tights, now that's a funny image!" This sounds complicated and time consuming, but if you let your imagination run a little wild, use Color, Action, Size, and Taste/Touch/Texture as your guide, you quickly add to your password creativity. More creativity means they will instantly pop into your mind, even weeks or months later. If you're struggling to remember more than the occasional password, add creativity and spend few extra seconds imagining the image or mental movie details.

6. **Inattention**. This goes hand in hand with several of the above issues, especially a lack of creativity. If you're pressed for time and rush through the password creation process, you're not going to remember it later when you need it. Remember "The Three Steps to Memory"? Get, Save, Recall. We have to pay enough attention during the password creation process to get the information into our minds. Part of the success with this entire system is that it forces you to stop and pay attention to your password. No longer can you create a new password in a few seconds using some variation of "fluffycat01". You take more time to create a memorable series of images, making yourself focus on your password. Between your natural ability to remember — when you try to — and the combination of a system and creative images, the passwords stick, like super

glue all over your fingers.

7. **Overdoing it.** If you attempt to change too many passwords in the same day or week, your mind may get overwhelmed, even with your effective system. Take it easy, follow the guidance above, and within a short time all your passwords will be more secure and memorable than ever.

Avoid these common problems. If you identify a different issue, or you're experiencing something you need help with, send me an email. I'm happy to help, and maybe it will help others in my memory presentations or future editions of this book. Brad@BradZupp.com.

**Replacing Passwords**

Don't replace your passwords all at once. We'll start out with a few and replace them little by little. Doing too many too quickly might overwhelm you, resulting in forgetfulness and discouragement. Over several days, you'll replace some of the most important ones, while testing yourself and your systems. As you succeed and prove to yourself that your systems are effective and passwords easy to recall, you will improve your cybersecurity.

There are several places where security is essential. We'll start with some of them, but a few need to wait until later.

- Your computer login. This is important because if someone gets into your computer, they can get into many websites if your browser is set to store your passwords for you. However, we will wait to replace (or add) a more secure password here. If you are unable to recall your login password for your computer, you may be in trouble and have to resort to taking it in for repair, or doing something drastic. Let's practice on something else first.

- Your email account. Second to your computer, this is probably the most important password. No matter how careful (or sweet) we are, I bet there's still something in an email you'd rather not have exposed to the entire world (or one particular person). As with the computer login, however, retrieving a forgotten main email password is difficult, so we'll skip this for now.
- Financial sites: online banking and investment accounts, credit card company website.
- Money and payment sites like PayPal.
- Social media websites, whether that's Facebook, LinkedIn, Twitter, or any other.
- Online shopping and e-commerce: Amazon, Esty, Ebay, etc.
- Work login.
- Work website.
- Cloud storage.
- Personal website or blog, especially WordPress.
- Food ordering and delivery sites.
- Travel websites like Priceline or Hotwire.

**Exercise #17: Your Social Media Account**

Start with your main social media website, because it's a huge, obvious target for hackers. If you don't have a social media account, you can either use this as another practice exercise or create one to see what all the fuss is about.

Use the system. When you think about Facebook, Twitter, Instagram, or your favorite site, what comes to mind? A particular "face" or a favorite "book"? The experience you have by being in touch with your friends and family such as "connection" or "love"?

That's your anchor. *Visualize it.* Don't merely think about it.

Use your preferred Password Creation Method next. Use AFSTR or APR.

Apply your capitalization, special character, and number replacement systems to create your final password.

Now the big step: login to your account and find the "Update Password" area. They may require you to enter your current password to change it. Hopefully you remember it. If not, go through the "Forgot Password" steps to have a new one emailed to you, login, and then change your password to the one created by your personal password system.

Here's the new next step. If your browser asks if you want it to save the new password, make a decision about that. It depends mostly on whether others have access to your computer, how trustworthy they are, and whether you travel with your computer (or if there are other chances for it to be lost or stolen). My default is to not allow my browser to save any login details for banks, investment accounts, e-commerce sites, or anywhere that stores my credit card. I allow it for social media, streaming music sites, and any others that aren't private or financial.

If you've made the decision that your browser will not save your password, *log out of the site immediately.* This will force you to input the password again while it's still fresh. This review of the password, as you type it in again, is the final step in both AFSTR and APR. It will help cement the password in your mind.

If you decide to have your browser store your password, *imagine* logging out of the site once again. **Literally close your eyes, visualize logging out, then logging back in. Type**

**your login name and password lightly on the keys of your computer or the screen of your device.** Imagine the word chain or phrase chain connections from anchor onwards, as well as the exact letters, characters and numbers you enter.

Logging out and then immediately back in (or imagining the process) may seem ridiculous, but this is a non-negotiable step. **Taking 45 seconds to log out and back in — either literally or mentally — is essential to helping retain the new password.**

The next time you take a break, use the restroom, or during your commute home, review your new password. "I changed my Facebook password using my new system. Now it's (fill in your password)." Review the special characters, the numbers, letters, and capitalization method. If you're alone, say it out loud.

Lastly, when you brush your teeth each evening before bed, ask yourself, "What passwords did I create or change today?" Use those two minutes productively to build those memory pathways.

This is the "Three Times Rule" (3x Rule) I use most frequently. I've found this is enough for me. In the beginning, you may also want to review the previous day's passwords again in the morning when you're brushing your teeth, or on your commute to work. Reviewing is a seemingly small step that makes a huge difference. My coaching clients and seminar attendees who skip or minimize this step are always the ones who complain that they just can't remember the new password. For password success, imagine logging out and back in at least three times, adding details each time.

If you haven't changed your Facebook or other primary social media password yet, do it now before continuing. Then complete the first step in the 3x rule.

## Break Time

Now it's time to take a break. If you're excited about changing more passwords, that's great. I still want you to wait at least one day before changing any other passwords.

## Day Two

Test yourself. Do you recall the new password from yesterday? Either login without using your browser's password recall feature, or close your eyes and imagine entering your password.

If you recall it perfectly and login with no problem, it's time to move on and change a few more passwords. Start with your most important websites, like you bank, investment, and e-commerce sites. Change a few now.

Avoid changing your email and computer login for another few days until you're 100% positive that you have perfect recall. Don't change more than three passwords per day to prevent your mind from being overloaded and risking confusing or forgetting each unique password.

If you're struggling, review the most common problems from the beginning of this chapter. Identify where you may be struggling and put a bit more effort into that area.

Continue updating your old passwords until all of them are ultra-secure and unforgettable. Use your system any time you login to a new website and have to create a password. Review each new password using the 3x Rule.

## Essential Passwords

Assuming you've successfully changed several website passwords and are feeling confident in your newfound abilities, it's time to look at changing other essential passwords: your computer login and email.

## Exercise #18: Change Your Most Important Passwords

1. Research how to retrieve your computer login password and your email password in the unlikely event you forget them. What are the steps? Know them before you start.

2. You must take extra time for any essential password that is difficult to retrieve. You don't have to make it more secure than your other passwords. Your system at this point should be quite robust. Use the same steps you have previously — don't adapt or change your system for these passwords, because that will make them harder to recall and more confusing: "Did I add those extra capital letters because it's my work email? Hmmm..."

3. Write it down. Yes, I know I said several times not to, but there are some passwords that are so important and so difficult to retrieve that you must write them down. We do occasionally forget even the most creative password. Accidents happen and our family, friends, or co-workers may need to access our systems. *Don't type the password into a file on your computer.* Write it down on a piece of paper, printed clearly, and put it in a secure, locked location that someone you completely trust knows about.

A fireproof, waterproof home or work safe may be perfect. For added security, put it in a sealed envelope with your signature over the seal, so you know if anyone ever opens it without your permission.

4. Change the password. Log out, then log back in. Do this between three and ten times, depending on how frequently you'll use it. If the password is for your computer login, you'll be using it frequently, so a few times to cement it should be fine. If it's for your email account, which you are most likely continuously logged into, be sure to practice it several times. It's horrible to need to access your email while traveling, or off-site in front of a client, and not recall your password.

5. Periodically log out and back in to practice your password. If you don't need to log out (your main email account, for example), practice it by pretending to login. Do this while the computer or phone is off, or just lightly touch the keys to simulate the login process. Review using the 3x Rule, or review more often for these essential passwords.

Wait at least a day, then repeat this process with any other essential passwords.

## Documentation

I recommend writing down several passwords and setting them aside for safekeeping, as mentioned above. If something horrible happens, your loved ones need access to your cyber life. Make it easy on them by having these essential passwords stored safely where they can access them in an emergency. As long as they have access to your computer (or phone and tablet), plus your email accounts, most passwords for websites can be easily reset via email. If the passwords are written down clearly, however, this step is saved and they are spared extra effort.

**Exercise #19: Document Essential Passwords**

If you haven't yet, write down the website, login name (or email), and password for the following:
- Computer login.
- All email accounts.
- Banking and investment websites.
- Blog.
- All social media sites.
- Any website your work manager or assistants, family, friends, or beneficiaries need access to if you are incapacitated.

# 14
## *Replacing Old Passwords and Other Security Ideas*

Experts disagree on how frequently old passwords should be replaced. Some say every few months, especially for shorter (12 characters or fewer) passwords. Others say that if you have a secure password, with plenty of characters (16+), keep it unless there is a reason to suspect it's been compromised.

Everyone agrees that if you receive notice from a website that has a security breach, or hear it on the news, then it's time to immediately update your password. (Be aware of phishing and spear phishing scams as mentioned earlier, however.) The best protection for a website security breach is to have completely different passwords for every single website or login. If one site is hit by hackers and its password/user name list is stolen, your accounts on other websites are safe because the password they got is only useful for the site they stole it from. If you're proactive about changing your password for that site promptly, the impact should be minimal.

### Replacing Old Passwords

There are many websites that automatically require you to update your password, sometimes as frequently as monthly or quarterly. What do you do then? You have a secure, 20-character password with numbers, upper- and lowercase letters, and special characters, yet you're being told it's time to change. The difficulty is being able to successfully delete your creative old anchor and links from your mind, then replace them with new images. This is tricky, because you've entered the password for a few months and it's already ingrained in your memory.

There are two approaches.

1. Keep the same anchor, but replace the links or phrase. If you have a strong anchor, this may be the approach for you. This also works best if the anchor for the website was difficult to create. Repeat the First link, Second link, Third link, and Review parts of AFSTR. Make sure all the new images are just as compelling as the old ones from the previous password. *Resist the temptation to make the old password the anchor, or base the new password on the old one in any way.* Eventually you'll have yet another new password. Using old passwords as anchors requires recalling more and more links over time. Go back to the original anchor and create a second set of links.

2. Replace the anchor and start fresh. Remember our Facebook example? What does "Face" remind you of, or what does "Book" remind you of? If you picked "Face" for the anchor the first time, switch the new anchor to "Book". If you picked "Friends" last time, pick "Family" this time. For the *SuperCheapo* website example, pick another friend notorious for being thrifty. In either case, make your first link an image that your new anchor reminds you of, then continue. If you're using the Phrase Chain Method, think of a new saying and convert it to a password.

With either approach, it's important to log out, then log back in. Practice typing the new password to erase the old and replace it with the new. Keep the 3x Rule in mind and review the new version during lunch, at the end of the day, or while brushing your teeth before bed.

## Cell Phone Passwords

Many people still do not lock their cell phones. For security, set your phone to lock when you aren't using it. Since anyone accessing your smart phone has direct access to your email, social media accounts, and more, a strong password is essential.

## Exercise #20: Create a Password for Your Cell Phone

Use at least eight numbers for your password. Avoid your or your friend's phone number, your birthday or year, or any other easily-guessed numbers or patterns for your password. Add a password, using either a number that you'll remember (but is hard to guess) or use the number chart from the Assigned Password System section to create a fun story. Practice it a few times while reviewing and adding details to your images. Note that this is an important password you don't want to forget, so write it down and store it securely as discussed previously, just in case.

## Two-Factor Authentication

Is it enough to have a personal password system and use it to create robust passwords that are easy for you to remember but hard for others to break? For most people, yes. But there are still other security measures you can take to make your cyber security stronger.

Microsoft, Twitter, Google, Apple, Facebook, and other sites now offer a way to protect yourself even more: two-factor authentication. If you have set up two-factor authentication, you need not only your user ID and password, but also another item to get access to the site or system: a short password that is generated randomly, then sent as a text message to your cell phone. You must enter this unique code each time you login to that site. Some only require a second authentication when you log on from a different device than usual, or a different IP address (computer location).

If hackers somehow have your user ID and password, they'd have access to the site that the password is for. If you have two-factor authentication set up, they wouldn't be able to access the site without also having access to your cell phone to receive the special code that is sent to it as a text message.

If you stay logged in, it's not as annoying as if you frequently log out and log back in. Imagine every time you access your online banking account, you enter your user ID and password, then wait for the bank to automatically text you your one-time password. Secure but potentially annoying, depending on how often you need to access that website. If you're using the systems from this book to create unique, long passwords for every website, you may choose to not use the two-factor authentication for all but the most important sites.

Remember, it's up to each of us to decide how secure we want our digital lives to be. Are you the type of person who leaves your keys in the car while spending the day shopping and seeing a movie in the mall, with all your valuables in plain sight? I doubt it, but if that's what you're comfortable with, I still encourage you to take more precautions in your online life.

On the other end of the spectrum, do you have more than two locks on each door? A monitored security system with armed response? HD security cameras? A guard dog? Are you a famous person, a public figure, a target for hackers, or have a job in law enforcement or politics? If so, you'll use every idea in this book, and two-factor authentication will be a welcome addition as well.

You may decide there are one or two websites that warrant this level of security. An online backup of your personal data, including pictures, or an email account used for private matters, might require two-factor authentication.

Since each site's process is different, I'll leave it to you to find and implement it. Set it up and use it for a welcome added level of security, but don't skimp on the main password. Use your personal password system to make it not only difficult to hack or guess, but also easy for you to remember.

## Exercise #21: Enable Two-Factor Authorization

Decide if there are any websites that require two-factor authentication. I suggest securing your main email address this way — the one that you use as a login for most websites. Your computer normally remains logged in to your email, so having a two-factor authentication shouldn't be annoying. Since someone gaining access to this account could then use it to reset all your other passwords, it's important to take extra precautions with it.

# 15
## *Afterword*

Your journey is complete. You've put effort into creating a personal password system, and it has paid dividends. You have a stronger memory and better cybersecurity. You've even improved your creativity.

Having a system makes it easy and possible to remember anything we set our minds to. Your personal password system makes it simple to create secure passwords that you easily remember. Keep using your system every time you need a new password. Enjoy how easy it is, and feel how nice it is to know you are more secure than ever before.

If you're interested in what the mind is capable of, consider this. I'm currently working on setting a world record, called The Pi Matrix Challenge. It has been called "The Everest of Pi Memorization Tests." It involves knowing not only the first 10,000 digits of Pi in five digit segments: 3. 14159 26535 89793... but also being able to instantly identify any of the segments. Judges will give me 50 random segments and I must be able to correctly recall the five digit segments before and after any given segment. This is timed, so I have to recall all of them perfectly in less than 16 minutes, 38 seconds to set a new world record. I've attempted it twice so far. The last time, I came so close to the record, but ultimately missed it. I plan to try again soon.

Just a few years ago, my memory for numbers was horrible. Now I can attempt an amazing feat of memory like the Pi Matrix Challenge. If I can go from where I was — unable to easily recall a phone number — to attempting world records, you can improve your memory enough to remember more secure passwords. Trust in the system you have created and keep practicing.

The last step in this process is helping others improve their password security. I'm sure you know of at least a few other people who struggle with remembering secure passwords. I need your assistance to get the word out about these methods. In the old days, reviews from a few big newspapers or magazines spread the word about a good book. Today, books rely on short reviews from more readers to get the word out. You have the power to help make other people's cyber security better. If you've enjoyed this book, please leave a short review on the site where you purchased it.

The review doesn't have to be much; other potential readers don't need a book report like we used to do in school. Just a few sentences. Did it make sense? Was it helpful to learn about cybersecurity? Did you learn about methods for creating more secure passwords? Was it enjoyable to read? Decently written? Who would you suggest read it? What did you like best about it?

Also, please consider mentioning it in a social media post. At the very least, help keep your friends and family secure from hacking. Post the title of the book, my name, and what you liked most about it. You can use this on almost any social media site, including *Yearly*, the exclusive site for people born the same year as you. (Do you remember the anchor you created for this site? What about the links or phrase you created?) Please contribute to making life easier and safer for your friends and family, and the world much more difficult for hackers.

If you struggle to remember names, birthdays, assignments, or what people talk with you about, consider looking into one of my webinars, self-study courses, or private coaching. Sign up for my free memory tips, announcements of upcoming events, courses, and books at www.BradZupp.com.

If you have a young student in your life, or want the basics of a better memory in a fun, easy-to-read book, please read my book for kids (adults love it too): *Unlock Your Amazing Memory: The Fun Guide that Shows Grades 5 to 8 How to Remember Better and Make School Easier.*

Be sure to read *Stay Safe: 99 Tips to Protect Yourself Online*, which is the companion book to this one. You can download it free at: www.BradZupp.com/bonus.

Finally, if you have any thoughts, questions, comments, or concerns, send me a note. Memory improvement is my passion, and I'm here to help. Email: Brad@BradZupp.com.

Thank you for reading.